Believe

the

Bird

Beth Wood

MEZCALITA PRESS, LLC
Norman, Oklahoma

Believe

the

Bird

Beth Wood

Table of Contents

Chapter 3: I Talk Back

Chapter 4: True Stories

Chapter 5: More Yes

Acknowledgements

I owe a debt of gratitude to Nathan Brown and Ashley Stanberry-Brown for steadfast belief in my work and my evolution, to Ann and Bob Wood for reading drafts and offering feedback, to Kim Stafford for inspiration and encouragement, and to my Patreon community for your belief in me and your direct support. Thank you to Sheri Williamson for the use of her beautiful Anna's Hummingbird image. Thank you to Lauren Hill for distilling the heart and message of this book into one vision for the cover. Thank you to all who read poetry and to all who believe in it and thirst for it like I do. I have joked around in the past by saying, "Poetry is important; I will die on that hill!" But I wasn't really joking. I'm just lucky I get to live on that hill, too.

"We tell ourselves stories in order to live."

~ Joan Didion

"When the bird and the book disagree,
believe the bird."

~ John James Audubon

Believe

the

Bird

To the Great Horned Owl in the Middle of the City Right Above My Friend Annie's Garage in the Elbow Crook of an Ancient Tree,

Thank you.
Sometimes I forget to look up.
I can't recall what caused me
to pause, stop, gaze skyward on
this particular August evening
between moving boxes and trying
to decipher what is actually inside
them. But I gasped at the sight
of you. I held my breath, *Oooooo*,
I squealed hopping on one foot,
silly with delight. Meanwhile you
blinked slowly and carried on as if
to say *remember not to get too excited*
about things, it makes people suspicious.
Touché. I ran in to tell Annie and
we both ran out to salute you and
gasp, already having forgotten your
advice. You blinked and posed the
same question again and again.
The sun fell asleep. Who makes
such delicious magic? Or is it all
around us all the time while we gaze
downward? Who makes the elbow
tree, the color of sky, the wind?
Who indeed.

Chapter 1:

Growing up Girl

ARCHER IN THE DARK

To call forth hope
one must pull taut the string
of a years-held dream, a plan laid bare,
a contentedness begun to rot.

She'll play the owning-blame game—
guilt for miles and miles
but then remember in the dark
in strong medicinal doses

the tangled logic that
brought her here. All in the
dead of night. All in stubborn
silence. It's in this gutted-

out room from which the call
must come. The bow, and
the arrow set carefully on fire—
not reckless; earned. Now point

that thing, aim high, and shoot.

DEFENDING SALT

I sprinkle it on everything.
Generous heapings of heavy,
fat crystals; I am in love with
its cause and effect. Luscious
flavor blooms on the surface,
dances in my mouth, shimmers
for a split second and is gone.
Perhaps I come from it, the way
my hair drinks in ocean water,
my skin, the buoyancy it lends,
holds me like tiny hands up and
down my earthly body, I crave it
like a dog licking wet sweaty skin.
Little tins in my purse, bowls in
my kitchen, shakers on the table,
blue cardboard box in the high
cupboard; it is once and for all
a healing thing. Even I know that.
Soak my bones. I swallow it, sing
my never-ending saltsong, taste the
memory once again of being whole.

GROWING UP GIRL

Do you think I'm beautiful?
You're built like a linebacker

Do you think I'm beautiful?
Your face is pretty but her body's slamming

Do you think I'm beautiful?
I would use the word 'curvy'

Do you think I'm beautiful?
You have those little lines around your lips

Do you think I'm beautiful?
Your hair is so…crazy

Do you think I'm beautiful?
You could tone things up a bit

Do you think I'm beautiful?
Your eyes are set so deep

Do you think I'm beautiful?
You have man hands

Do you think I'm beautiful?
You should smile more

Do you think I'm beautiful?
Your tits are too heavy

Do you think I'm beautiful?
Your tits are too small

Do you think I'm beautiful?
Your skin is a minefield

Do you think I'm beautiful?
You have a bubble butt

Do you think I'm beautiful?
You're just not my type

Do you think I'm beautiful?
You have resting bitch face

Do you think I'm beautiful?
Your teeth are crooked

Do you think I'm beautiful?
You don't photograph well

Do you think I'm beautiful?
Those red moles are everywhere…little pin pricks

Do you think I'm beautiful?
The phrase 'thunder thighs' comes to mind

Do you think I'm beautiful?
You're too old

Do you think I'm beautiful?
YES

Wait, what?
YES

Are you sure?
YES

I don't believe you.
OK

But thanks.

FIRE AND DUST

Highway sign says
Dangerous Curves
and I laugh out loud

You're damn right
they are, I think,
and I'm not sorry
anymore.

What kind of place
would teach its young
girls to hate the soft
roundness of their
ripening bodies? Who
would trade in on
blind obedience?

Such shame to spend
my first forty years of
woman-ness hating
the shell I was in—

shame indeed. Now
I take that shame and
chain it—never mine
to begin with, just a
hungry, mean, teeth-
baring street dog that
followed me home.

He's dead now. I
buried him in the
yard, said a little
prayer as I raised
the shovel, thanked
him for what he
showed me, baptized
him in fire and dust,
walked away clean.
But I'm laughing, and
now I can't stop. It's
cruel, I know, death
is never funny; but I was
clean to begin with,
all along.

LET'S BE HONEST

In the morningdark
I dress for confusion,
sometimes for delight—

these two see-saw
sisters bringing me
dreams, stories, an

endless succession of
scenes in a movie I
never bought a ticket

for, swell of violins,
arc of tension, then
release. My oddness

is distilled into hard
proof of itself as days
march calmly on.

Women all around
me pour poison on
their heads, inject

cow meat into their
lips, eyebrows, faces,
sagging breasts, tuck

and squeeze, anything
to stop time, diminuendo
on a score I've never

managed to see. I
would rather conduct
a symphony of trees.

THE ROPES

You forget your animal self
and it has left you tipsy, un-
abridged, about to spill over
into tomorrow. The next thing
comes and you fall into it—
a hole in the ground, a non-
sensical love, a snap decision,
lightning bolt come and gone.
Dazed and bemused is your
modus operandi, sometimes
you forget to breathe. Flash
to the Missouri cowboy calm-
ing horses—that brittle polio
limp just something he wore
but never took off. They sighed
out silver clouds in bitter high
mountain morning cold as he
hummed *Eeeeeeeasy* and patted
flanks. Each time they forget a
little. *Easy now.* Forged out of
electricity, born ready to run,
drunk on the promise of new
grass, young evening sun, never
quite solving the mystery of
where the ropes come from.

GIRLS AND HORSES

What IS it with girls and horses?
asks the man with a crown on
the high-up hill who probably never
had dirt beneath his fingernails, who
hides up in his castle spinning yarns.
A question so rhetorical, so loaded
and plumb like *what IS blue?* that my
head whirls away into another plane.
Well... I say, and no matter how far
back I reach I cannot find words.
Only clear sky, tall sighing grass,
leaning barns, iridescent swallows
writing cursive poems in evening
air, coarse white hair wet with sweat
caked in dirt, long dancing braids,
dinner about to be set on the table
and called, two ears pointing forward
like sails, windfingers ruffling my wild
dandelion hair, the blessed hallelujah
of unshorn hooves delivering me to
a world without machines. *Hmmm, I
don't know,* I say out loud while chewing
on my secret—one so sweet I am still
tasting it all these years later. I sigh
and shrug, knowing I'll never tell.

So Many Ways: Here Is One

If you'd like to practice
being invisible, try being
a middle-aged woman in
a guitar shop! It's so easy
you could almost shoplift
(even though you would
never do that, your mama
taught you right). Here's
one: try taking one of the
more expensive models off
the wall—one from way
up high—and watch them
wonder how it got down
all by itself. Play scales,
tease out a few licks, and
if you really want to blow
some minds, buy something.
I once had a highly-educated
man, a mentor, tell me he
didn't see how it is different
for a woman. In music, that is.
(Right after I had explained
how it was.) I blinked into
my coffee, flummoxed, let it
hang in air there for a minute,
my disbelief like a swarm of
angry bees buzzing around my
tired head. I get dizzy now just
thinking about it. Well of course
he doesn't see. I am invisible.

I WISH FOR YOU

I wish for you
a joy that feels like
returning,

the hopefulness of
a seed
planted deep, sleeping.

I ache to know
the why, I ache
to know that the why

is not mine to know.
I ache to see
the burned-out light bulb

she could never reach
and wonder how long
she lived in partial darkness—

although some grandmothers,
no doubt, can make
biscuits in the dark.

I wish for you
such steady hands, blind
knowing, unhurried faith.

I wish for you
a joy that feels like
returning.

Chapter 2:

Heart Like A Bird

Truth And Vine

Just as ripe blackberries hold
the sun, a lover's body holds
the verb of loving: the doing,
the expanding hopefulness
of each honeyed kiss. Bodies
knowing what they know forget
their thirst, and then it storms
back in—a season with hands
reaching for everything not
tied down. Hearts are more
forgetful: clumsy, animal-soft,
prone to bruising, bent on the
vine toward asking, all at once
gleaming, tangled, dew-soaked,
thorn-bound. Reach a hand in
to learn truth on the vine. Go
in easy, wear gloves, begin.

BRAMBLES

It would feel strange
if there weren't at least
one bullet hole on this
railroad crossing sign

or one flattened snake
on this blacktop highway

or one thousand bright
faces of flowers that my
aunt's garden club ladies
call *Road-sidea.* And here

a snarl of blackberry
brambles, endless tangle
of vine, thorn, balled
up into a deadly mess—

always a tiny rustle of
something living within.

Same with borders,
same with the heart.

THE BARGAIN

Love makes us forget
(but not the everyday kind).
Grand electric gesture of a
first kiss, slippery howling
birth, last whispered words.

Sometimes music,
sometimes snow,
that one foggy night a
coyote called out and you
stood bathed in moon-
light without clocks.

Then next we say yes,
such elaborate scaffolding
we have invented to live
under: the bargain. That
upon which we agree
remains an unspoken
nod from each to each.

An ambulance screams
then flies by, its cries
bending in right angles
in just-before-dawn air.

The best we can hope for:
an ordinary sun, that our
yesterdays become todays,
then tomorrows, then
yesterdays again.

Reading The News

Restless Mind Still Swims

Late Night Dinner Still Churns

Pitch-Black-of-3:03-Clock
Still Laughs When I Sigh

Morning Still a Miracle:
Birds Still Cheerful a Little Too Early

Dog Still Snoring at My Side:
Tail Thumping When I Reach Down

Coffee Still A Revelation

Words Still Kites, Blankets, Life Rafts

Body Still Astonished, Grateful
for Another Chance to Feel,
Taste, Run, Make Something

Heart Like a Bruise, Heart
Like a Bird, Heart Like a
Flower, Flowing River, Song

THE ALWAYS-HUNGER

Will the heart ever learn?
I wonder. Who can
know? There are some-
times whispers of truth,
if I am quiet. Trying to
hold back water is its own
particular kind of foolish-
ness, says sideways-tipped
wren in the morning rain.

Will it ever un-learn?
perhaps is the better
question. Will it melt
into forgiveness, which
cannot be earned? Will
it hoard and fortress an
imagined truth in service
to the hunger, the always-
hunger, even when fed?

I long for a simple life.
Birdsong, high grasses,
cleansing rain. Mercy that
can only be found in the
deep eyes of a friend. Gentle
wisdom, fidelity of an old
dog snoozing in the half-light,
running circles in dreams,
waiting for the day to begin.

SET THE TABLE

If the stars had been
any brighter we would
have tripped over them.
If the evening had been
any more soft, any more
forgiving, we could have
bowed and said amen—
your sleepy garden singing
to us in deep colors, in
exhaled breaths, a crow
in the distance, dogs curled
underfoot like seashells.
If you reached your hand
out in the dark and placed
it on mine, my hand would
say yes, and thank you for
the reaching. Meanwhile, at
that very moment something
else slips away, someone
grieves; the spark between
our fingers a benediction—
the way two old painters
who have no answers
say grace.

There Are No Wrong Seasons

Says Mary of the pines,
Mary of the heron, Mary
of the double hurricane.
There is only a blank canvas
of time, and perhaps not even
that the way we see it—our
human knowing just a silly
game, a clumsy unravelling,
we upright corvids with our
squawky opinions, sneaky
logic, arrogant thumbs. I
didn't know it was May, or
December for that matter,
but here we are. Here is your
hand on my cheek, my mouth
on your mouth, your tongue
stamping my impatient skin.
Tattoo of all I thought to be
true right here on my breast,
beam from my eye to yours.
Go on and suck the nipple
taut, let us sing the delicious
friction of calloused hands on
milky skin: these days I'm
prone to wintering; help
yourself to spring.

LIKE IT IS

A steady drumbeat
led me to that place on
the outskirts of town
like some subconscious
subterranean marching
order, playing like I had
a choice. I knew it the
second I set foot there.
I noticed it in tree limbs,
let it run just under my
skin quick, magnetic,
male. I played like I had
a choice (like all good
fools do). When I quit
playing there were no
masks, heart beating on
granite—bare, mineral
and animal all at once.
Now I play with shapes,
round the corners, note
the heat, the infinite soft-
ness, this tender miracle,
living thing grown wild
between us. I paint with
words. Call it surrender.
Call it like I mean it. Call
it wellspring, clear water.
Call it windfall. Call it ever-
ness, call it oh-my-god. I'll
go ahead and call it love.

YOU WERE BEAUTIFUL THEN

tucked into a dark corner
I had prescribed and you
had found, wide shoulders
hunched over a book
with whiskey.

Who am I to disturb this?
I thought right before
I walked in to borrow
your eyes—further, who
am I to disturb any

thing—each moment
curling up like wood
shavings under a plane
rising round, falling
away without sentiment.

You were beautiful then
by a different fire—
easy laughter while I
tucked my toes for
warmth under the
weight of you

and closed my eyes
drinking in delicious-
ness, at the same time
wondering how this
particular spell would
end: small riot

of geese flying high
under moonlight, wood
gone to ash.

It is the most human
thing I can think of:

to swallow
a question mark.

TO THE WATER

I go to the water
when a man breaks my heart.
I sink down effortless,
weightless, held.

When a man skips town
I might bring whiskey.

All this time
this whirling world had me
thinking I was weak,
broken, tossed.

Driftwood for certain but—
such magnificent shores.

Such dangerous beauty,
the turning wheel, every
little corner alive with
something unnamed, wild.

Tides come and go. The
heron on stilts sees all
from on high, makes
no sound.

Untethered, bruised, alone
like the day I was born
I go to the water.
I am unmade,
made again.

ENOUGH

The water has personality, she
says, and I say hmmmm,
skeptical of her retelling
of a story I already know.
This picture window an
invitation, a call impossible
not to answer if you can
get still enough. *Sit still,
listen,* it says, *let lovers have
their day.* Ah yes, I thought
so. *Tell me one word?* I ask
the bluegrey oracle now.
Enough it says. It is the
answer to everything.

Chapter 3:

I Talk Back

FLIP-SIDE SUPERNOVA

On the flip-side of desire
is rot, moss, ash. How did
we get here? you might ask
yourself and you'd be right.
When we were a tumbling
mass of hair and sweat and
blushing skin could you have
imagined this? Your father's
acid rage a brute truth I never
bargained for. And where I
thought I had none, I have
currency now. In every word,
every letter, every breath: *I
will not pay for this.* Although
by my loss I pay, I keep the
change. I have since learned
a much better use of my one
sovereign heart. I have made
a place here in the dirt where
I can tend tender sproutings
of seed, a life. From my knees
I've struck a new bargain—
this time I'm the one burning,
this time I may never stop.

QUICK BIRDS

I talk back.
Sass like I never have before
and it lands like a slap on his barely-whiskered face.

All the times
before of softening, molding
my shape, tucking in, holding my tongue on a leash.

You're losing it,
he says, and I say, *I know.*
A kind of unraveling come home to roost.

Then I stop,
leave the game behind—the dance,
feel green fingers of breeze in my hair, sun rising

up like courage
sprouting from seed. *Never again,*
I whisper underbreath, *I will not pay the price,* and yet

we all do.
Men with their anger, violence,
acting-out, shame-shifting, fists, walls, words, cocks,

guns for peace—
they say don't worry, it's much
safer this way—armed to the teeth and snoring.

You're too sensitive,
his broken record mouth says and
this time I stifle a laugh like a cough in church. Stuck

in my throat
this new truth and the words fly
from there unadorned, black darting birds at dusk.

Call the doctor
he says, *you're having a mid-life crisis.*
The dog raises his ears, looks from that tight mouth

straight to me
then back to him, cloudy old-dog
eyes following those quick birds around the room,

brown head never
moving, bless his old-dog heart. *You're
damn right I am,* I say, and I'm just now getting started.

HANDLEBAR

You're too sensitive
says the man who makes
promises then breaks them.

You're too mean
I think but never
say it out loud

because I'm sensitive.
His crooked mouth
slanting toward a thousand

sad tomorrows. Anything
that you wouldn't say
out loud to my father

you don't get to say
to me. His face would
show the cracks in

your story, the weak,
all-too-familiar angry-male
places and he might

pinch his own arm
to keep from laughing.
He's not the warring

kind. My friend's dad
is a real cowboy. Probably-
cleans-his-teeth-with-a-

knife cowboy. Handlebar
mustache, calloused hands,
felt hat and all. Let's see

what he does with
the *you always's* and
you never's. I've seen

him shot-gun shoot
a tin can from a
fence on horseback.

I've seen him rise before
dawn, ride up a mountain,
do what must be

done, come home, re-
move the dust and armor,
wrap his wife in kisses.

I've seen what he does
with snakes. What was it
again you were saying?

INVENTORY

For the record I am not
your play-thing,
your punching bag,
your blank white screen.

I am not your doll,
your excuse,
your moral compass,
your mirror on the wall.

I am not your trophy,
your pin-up,
your wrecking ball,
your ever-after,

the stone to break you open.
I am not the reason.
I am not the glue,
the cruise-director,

the cook,
the maid,
your oracle,
your secretary.

I am not a distraction,
a healing balm,
a band-aid,
a boomerang,

I am not the sun.
I am not a mouse,
a spider,
a dog begging for scraps.

I am not your mother,
your father,
your ex-wife,
your damsel-in-distress.

I am not your project,
your problem,
your whip,
your warm blanket.

I am not a saint.
I am not your surveillance,
your nurse,
your dumping ground,

your endless well,
your vessel for complaints.
I am not a fantasy,
a punch-line,

a drug,
a doormat,
a scapegoat.
I am not your angel.

I am not your shrink,
your interpreter-of-dreams,
your guide through
the wilderness,

your conscience,
your free-pass vending machine,
your road-map
to happiness.

You might be wondering
what then I am doing here
because I am not
your anything.

I am myself.
Wholly and only.
None other than flesh
and blood woman

tending and feeling,
dreaming and waking,
holding firm at the center,
come to set this straight.

I've come to make a claim.
For the record I am not
your night watchman,
your 911 call,

your alarm, but you
could take a look around:
your house is on fire,
and I am not your water.

To a 21ST Century Man: An Inquiry

You had to have it.
Go after it like gang-
busters, full court press.
Plant a flag, lay claim
to a living heart, then
resent its beating.

You pull her close.
Reel her in to that tight
spot where you block the
sunlight between the
cracks of your pulsing
bodies. Seal it real good,
then complain you can't
see in the dark like that.

You use words like *only*
and *great love* and *second
time around.* You sprinkle
in a sigh or two. O how
you needed this, thank
God or Universe or Great
Mercy you finally found it,
then you scoff and recoil
at her needing.

I'm not saying you're
a bad person, I'm just
tired. And there are other
ways. I'm wondering
in this century of two

thousands if you could
gentle the horse a little.
Find a way to love
without conquering.

SALT

Well I have heard of a lot of things but not this.
The deep, wide net of betrayal pulling me under now.
It's another world down here – the quiet alone
enough to rewire forty-seven years of thought rivers.

Where there seems to be a ghost, there is a ghost.
I know that now, being the ghost herself.
Almost like I never existed – except for the
inconvenient fact of my breasts, bone, pulsing blood.

Except for every sigh I gave – each one true.
Truth being unfamiliar to you, now I see how it is
too unbending for your arsenal – so it is shifted,
bartered, sung, veiled, scrapped, defiled, wasted.

The pile here at the bottom of the deepdark sea.
A dark so deep it yawns and swallows, then sleeps.
I swim to shore, I swim to freedom – I swim toward what
is real. Covered in salt, I unghost myself. I unlove you.

REALITY TV

I have grown bone tired
of that sleepy old metric:
disheveled, mop-haired,
pitifully unshaven and
unkempt baby-man
stomping his gnarly feet
shouting, *but I'm important!*
his cigarette-soiled fingers
hanging limp at his side,
dead snake at his center,
making the whole world
slave to his appetite. To
mistake desperation for
eloquence when they're
not even in the same key:
how cliché. Oh Maestro,
alert the media. Just like the
old days I have to get up
to change the channel.

TAPDANCE

If you say it loud
you are too scary

if you say it quiet
you are too timid

if you don't say it
you are conniving

if you forget to say it
you are daft

if you rewrite it
you are a bitch

if you sing it
you are witchy

if you wail it
you are just crazy

if you mean it
you become yourself

FORTY-SEVEN

In my class he snorts, stomps,
grumblegrumbles like a billy-goat,
enough to make us collectively
chair-shift and roll our eyes.

He ribs me: *well easy for YOU to say,*
YOU didn't have to DO the exercise;
he balks at careful instructions,
he even nose-breathes out loud.

When asked to share his work he
hems, haws, passes. *I told the director*
you're so PRETTY, randomly lodging
a pebble in my shoe for the duration.

But what IS a melody? he bloviates
and exactly how is writing a song different
than writing a sonnet? My middle-aged
students heavy-sigh like teenagers.

Out of mercy the trees also sigh.
Toward the end of night when all
writers are full-bellied and full of
hope and heart, starting to scatter,

he suddenly stands up, looks my
way, says *Thanks for the book, kid!*
and stumbles into the darkness.
I am forty-seven years old.

BALANCE

God is a red-tailed hawk—
circling, soaring, sun-soaked;
not, I hate to tell you, a man.
A temper-tantrum-throwing,
jealous, bearded angryman
who p-r-e-s-i-d-e-s, around
whom we all tiptoe and scurry
like ants, underneath whom
we s-u-f-f-o-c-a-t-e. I will not
bow down, beg for mercy, pray
to let him into my heart, he who
starts wars. In fact, let's just say
it: put your swinging dick back
in your pants, good sir. Don't
get me wrong, I look up. But
my god is not a conqueror. She
dances with thermals, governs
telephone wire, takes only what
she needs, pens elaborate letters
in the sky, lands, squawks, turns,
regurgitates, folds hot wings. And
here's a revelation: she asks. To tell
you the truth, I pity the thirsty old
man, his power fading day by day by
unending day, surely he must feel it,
every star made to burn out, every
sun. It must haunt his long shivering
nights, one can certainly sympathize.
Balance, she whispers. Now, I think,
we are finally getting somewhere.

Chapter 4:

True Stories

Quiet Woman Drops a Coin on a Bus

She had lived a hundred
lives before—
time's red silk scarf
unraveling each one

so that the petal of a rose
shouted *echo*

so that ruby lips
became invocation

each one whispering to her
in dreams
all the while another
was being formed

hungry child
lover
mother
beggar
healer
minister of truth
wailer of grief

a hundred things you could
have asked but never do.

You never even notice her.
She bends to touch the
floor, limb of a willow.

Meanwhile you sigh, one
hundred lives of your own
weighing on your chest.

The horizon curves toward
tomorrow, yields, makes way
yet again for something new.

HONEYSUCKLE DARLINGS

Where I grew up, it was just
a weed muscling up over tops of
fences like there was something
to prove. Us kids walking home
from school would stop, drink
a single drop of nectar, skip on
to the next thing telling stories and
limping like peg-leg pirates. Home
by four when mom would call
just to make sure. I found some
the other day on Ainsworth Street—
sweet smell coming in ten feet before
sight all green and white and gold.
How far away now from those days,
those darlings. I tried to explain it to
you once—the ubiquitous aroma, the
pucker-faced sweetness. Innocent bees
drunk on their luck of finding it. If you
get over there, stop and see, will you?
Pull that white thread up and out and
taste, just like I said. You might just
remember something you never knew
you knew. You might then recognize
what I've been saying all along.

HOW TO CHOOSE A MOTHER

Get quiet. I mean, inside-of-a-
dark-cave quiet. Imagine a being
whose arms can carry you, then
let you go when it is time. Watch
her face when she receives any
kind of good news, see her eyes
light up from the inside: fireworks.
This is how she will feel about you
although you have never met. You
can sometimes see into her dreams
at night, the way she worries and it
feels like weight. She may even feel
small. But she will grow her courage
into a parachute so big, so unfailing
you can all fall without crashing. She
even knows secrets from when she
chose her mother, and they sound
like familiar music, like humming.
Like an endless river and you dip
your hand in, splash your face. It is
clear now. You close your eyes, fold
into yourself, swim your way in, count
the days one by one, watch the sky
go white, cry until at last you meet.

GRANDMOTHER SONG

Her hands smelled of onion and
pretty lotion—given, never bought.
She knew best where the wasps
lived, built their tumorous nests,
what to do when stung. Scorpions
are more difficult to predict—one
in her nightgown, one in her shoe,
one tucked behind the skillet, well
for heaven's sake. Make the bis-
cuits anyway. Her white downy
soft hair a crown for a queen with
no servants, no butler, no parade,
but still every living thing knew it.
Even now I bow down. From my
knees on the ground I hear the
stunned ruffled bird of her stifled
voice—she had a song. Sang it
through the cracks, wielding meat
tenderizer for stings and the sharp
scalpel of cruelty hiding behind
every dark corner. She tucked her
wings, sang it soft, hummed in our
ears, sheltered us all, sang it anyway.

Dear Carole & Nessa,

I'm not sure how to tell you this
but I'll just try: here I am the human
fumbler, the clumsy rambler, the
girl from the arid flatlands who still
marvels at every tree, every blossom,
every high hill. I watch in wonder
at your grace, your carriage, your
heads lifted in song even as they
bow heavy in grief. I see now there
can be both at once; before I was
an either/or person: I am changed.
A rose rises toward sun, shoulders
the weight of another afternoon.
What I want to give you is never
enough, what I want to tell you a
jumbled-up blackberry bramble of a
thing, what I want to do: impossible.
The world has shifted, and I see the
miracle of how it won't swallow you
up. But if there is one tiny moment in
the middle of one dark night when
you ache, when you wonder if you
can go on, my hand will be there
and I will reach back. You know
I'm up anyway. I can't take away
your pain but I can witness it, I can
sing, I can stand on a high green hill,
I can hold a ripe flower up to the sun
and say your names. Love always,

B

MARY OLIVER GOES TO SONG CAMP

She pulls in, says hello, signs the release form and takes her packet. She wanders among the tall trees looking up, pitches a tent in the shade down by the garden. She doesn't much mind the rooster—what seems to unravel in some remains solidly intact inside of her, her steady clockwork heart beating like a tiny muffled drum. She is relieved to learn on her first day that she does not have to be good. She writes ditties by the sea, marvels at the moon on dark water, its sing-song tides, drinks one beer by warm light of campfire before playing her song about her dog much to the delight of us all. Four of us feel the tug of memory until the next song about speed-dating causes us all to forget. She is quiet but friendly, appreciative of quick laughter, beautiful food, the abundance offered. Her life is wild and precious, and she knows it. And here she is while the wild geese fly over, doing something with it.

ROOM ENOUGH

Yes, I know there is
a spider in my bathroom
tucked in the corner

over there by the window.
I've tried vacuuming up
her work several times, how

it gleams in the sunlight.
She just rebuilds: weaver,
survivor. I don't have

the heart to do it to her
again; there is room
enough for both of us.

THE NIGHTHORSE

When I heard about the nighthorse
I didn't believe it. My leather-handed
rodeo-cowboy friend tried to explain it
one night over sushi; in the same sitting
he also told me the little green clump
of wasabi was green-tea ice cream, his
eyes flashing with big-brotherly delight
when I took a bite. He never tried to kiss
me and there was a certain freedom in it,
a question hanging gently between us like
a spider web once you decide to let it be,
let her weave in peace. My astonishment
took many forms that night: new silk of
raw flesh on my tongue, the deep ribbon
red of it, being a girl from the plains I had
no frame of reference for this pleasure. *No,*
he said, *it's a real thing. They have another kind
of sight, a deeper one, and you can sleep sitting up
while they carry you home.* I head-tilted and said
Really? and he nodded and grinned, divine
trickster. Just that day I had seen him set
a prayer wheel spinning. *So kind of like God?*
I asked, funny words from an unbeliever to
a prayer-spinning, sushi-eating cowboy. His
eyes just then did not slip: they said *Yes.*
They held the rope.

NOCTURNE IN D MINOR
for Chuck McDowell

When the late evening sky
offers up its best falsetto,
we tingle with delight

and say *aha yes! Again
please, again.* Sun on its
way to being forgotten

echoes the slippery-rock
rhythm of us, the river-
speaking story of us,

the ever-turning wheel.
We hardly ever
think to say *stay here*

because the irrepressible
sky says *I'll go now.* And
so it goes: at last

the nocturne in d minor
come for us; the curtain,
the empty theater chairs.

THE OLD WOMAN AND HER SECRETS

Most likely the good people of
this town have no recollection of her
as anything other than a blue-hair
drive-slow, always-pay-in-cash
cafeteria-goer who buys birdseed
by the twenty-pound sack, who
remembers bank holidays always,
who just got a new bug light.
Most likely they have no idea
how she was the youngest smartest
somewhat surprised sweetheart
beauty queen the county had ever
seen—like a horse-whip—and
no one knew what to do with
that part, not even her. Days die
away the same for all of them,
winter hoarding precious hours of
daylight. She stretches the phone
line to her bedroom and waits
again for nothing to happen.

TO THE FULL-BEARDED, BARREL-CHESTED MAN DOING TAI CHI ON THE EMPTY BASEBALL DIAMOND AT THE PARK BY MY HOUSE IN THE MIDDLE OF THE DAY,

Thank you.

I thoroughly enjoyed
your lumberjack ballet.

I can see you holding
firm at the center,
leaning forward
toward tomorrow.

I imagine you've never
used your fist as a hammer—
or even an exclamation point
for that matter. I breathe
deeper without knowing why.

Although I could
be wrong—I'm always
imagining things.

It could be you're just
trying something new
on lunch break. Or it
could be you see your
fists as silks—and you
just like dancing with
the wind. Either way,

thanks. You took me
somewhere today.

Keep doing you,

B

What To Say About Santa

has become topic of
frequent conversation
around tables of late—

my friends all mothers
and fathers to dimpled,
hopeful, spun-sugar-haired

children, December
creeping in. It is
hard to sit with

the discomfort of it,
the shades of ambiguity,
the outright lying.

How could a tiny
person not feel
betrayed? Or—

perhaps it could feel
special, even delicious
to be in on something?

Truth is it just gives
a name, a round shaking
belly, a beard and a suit

to this dance we do:
Hand over all the
hope we have

(what we can find
at least on any
given day). Sigh

knowing odds are
stacked against it
for the keeping.

TO THE LADY AT THE REC CENTER PRACTICING HER MOONWALK IN THE MIRROR OF THE GROUP EXERCISE STUDIO RIGHT BEFORE MY CLASS BEGAN,

Thank you.
I know Christmas is coming on.
So much to do, ready for, fuss
over. Red and green ribbons
everywhere, even at the gym.
I imagine you're getting ready
for a houseful. It really does
light up when they're all in it.
I'd like to think you're practicing
to show your grandkids. I like to
imagine them squealing with un-
bridled delight: *No, no, no Gamma,*
THIS is how you do it! I love how
there is hope in it, even if it is
the outdated kind. Even if you
never show them, or if you're
tired of Christmas, or if they don't
exist at all, I still say thank you.
Just now watching you I floated
to the top of that silly tree, high-
fived the angel, felt weightless
small and free for a tiny little
while. It was better than any
thing with a shiny ribbon on it.

Keep doing you,

B

CORGI AT THE PARK

Yes, there is despair.
There is cruelty beyond
all imagining. There is fire,
flood. There are flying bullets,
tyrants, hearts tangled in nettles
of bramble, barbed wire, thorn.
There is uncertainty, shame,
wounded pride, shedding
of skin, walking thousands
of dust covered miles just to
take back your own name.
But there is a corgi at the
park with a wheelchair
chasing a red bouncing ball,
and that alone is enough
to keep on going.

Chapter 5:

More Yes

ALL AT ONCE

There will be blood
in the most unlikely places—
scars rendered from on high,
down below, sideways. From
a cheese grater this morning
before light, the always-folly
of rushing in the presence of
sharper things. The time it takes
to realize you have been cut,
the deep sigh. This afternoon
in class a man marveled out
loud at the woven-ness of it all:
the syrupy rise and fall of the
orchestra rehearsing; bright
shimmering leaves; kids playing
outside in crystalline autumnal air
scattering squeals of joy. *It's all
happening at once!* he exclaimed—
stunned, unbelieving. We all
nodded and I wondered what
unnamed grief he carried, what
sorrow led him here to this old
schoolhouse room full of poets
and sharp light. What seesaw, what
counterweight? The way you feel
your pulse where the wounds are.
A silent pause lingered affirming
the plainness of it all, and the
wonder, happening all at once.
Yes it is, we said, and it was.

RECIPE

Memory, it seems,
is a knife blade—
treacherous, silent, quick,

and before you know
it there is blood. Try
not to get it

in the food. Reach
all the way back
for some salt-water,

a distant wave of joy.
Forgive your hands. Go
on, feed the living.

If Words Could Talk

How tempting to complain
about wiry white hairs sprouting
from my crown, to decry dry brittle
popping of knees, hips, the occasional ankle.

How natural, if not somewhat
cliché, to try and run harder, faster
against the clock. How delicious to moan,
my youth is over underbreath while turning calendar

pages, how brutal their neutrality, al-
most like they don't care. William Stafford's
first book of poetry was published when he was
forty-six. *Shut up and write*, those words say. And I do.

LAST WORDS

My poetfriend writes poignant musings
inspired by famous people's last words.

I'm trying to imagine what my last words
might be, should this be my very last breath—

probably something like, *That goddamned fly is
still in here. Hell, forget everything I've ever said.*

VESPERS

It takes a kind of courage
to notice small things. Is
there a silent river flowing
just beneath our feet? One
that holds everything that
ever happened? And one
above our heads with words
in it, songs? A great forgetting
and a great remembering
at the same time. Birds off
the script making an entrance,
helicopter seeds on the wind,
burning question of a rose.
A great soft hand saying *here*—
I made this puzzle for you.

HARVEST

Underneath sorrow runs
the joy-current—
sun peeking out behind

clouds,
milk on the edge
of souring.

How long can we
get by with just
one smile from
a stranger?

How often can we
turn to a ripe peach
amid our suffering?

The possibilities
infinite, woven.
Fabric of night sky,
flanks of sweaty horses,
cold spring from
a quiet mountain,

every tiny little
wonder a prayer,
an offering

meaning every-
thing and nothing
at the same time—

plumb fruit, just
now ripe for
the picking.

COYOTE COMMUNION

There are avenues we never
speak of—worn pathways carved
out by longing, time, gravity. Skin
glowing yellow from this smiling
campfire, trickster smoke chases
one thought after another around
and around until almost every one
of us has sat in that red chair. And
oh there is song—that magnificent
river of melody that lives in bones,
skin, hair, hands. A tired troop of
kindreds, we recognize each other
in passing—deeply so here, now.
Cold wanders in. I see him sitting
hunched and weary, resting a tired
back but laughing and I want to ask
aren't you lonely? but I can't find how.
We wander dark roads like coyotes,
doubling back where the eating is
good, howling with each other in
the night. Tenderness may never
come for me, I think, but it hangs
soft in shadows here, causes wind
to change. I grieve it like a missing
limb. My eye catches his for a split
second—the ripe golden glow now
gone to threads; we agree without
words that freedom has a cost—a
deep one. We pay in solitude, blood,

lost avenues, howling questions. This
sharp sky laden with impossible stars
answers back: we double down again.

ONE BEAD

It is hard, the poet said,
to string one bead at a time,
and my head nodded on its
own accord, I sighed deep
into my seat. Yes, it is hard
and that one moment in time
preserved in the amber of
my imperfect memory still
brings the sting of a tear for
the truth of this, the telling.
It is hard, yes, to string one
day, one breath, one sentence,
one outstretched hand at a time
when sometimes it feels there
can be no more. It is hard to
move one cord of wood. But
a fire in winter is a welcome
guest. It is hard to string one
memory at a time behind, hard
to realize memory is not straight
lines but balled up wires and what
can you do but laugh and shake
your head thinking this will
never come undone. It is hard
to laugh sometimes and yet then
hard to cry. But what other way
can there be? What rhythm, what
balm, what holy song but one tear,
one word, one bead at a time.

Peanut Gallery

Let me put it this way: there will be
those for whom your largeness will
be a problem, who will attempt with
squinted raptor eyes to shrink you
down to size, who will stand with
balled up fists and curse your light.
Let them. It is hard for a bruised up
shrivled up heart to come back from
its dry season. It will or it won't. Mean-
while, set the table. Laugh, eat, savor,
burn with secrets, share, shine, love.
It's what you were born for. More yes.

THE SOUL'S AGENTS
(title borrowed from Stephen Dunn poem)

We want you to be free.

We want laughter—deep laughter—
the kind that dissolves ugliness.

We want you to awaken
with the spark of something
just under your tongue.

We want you to laugh
at lies and how they
make us children.

We want you to know
we are all children.

We recommend a good book,
dinner with a friend,
playing cards on a snowy day.

We see how you trip and fall
and how you rise;
but there is blood, you say
and we say *yes.*

Watch the transformation
of years on a body, how you
will all but melt back
into the center.

But do not wait for death—
it is a door, but not
the kind you think.

You may expand into
who you are any time.

We'll be waiting.

WHAT REMAINS

One day you will hear
music that reminds you
of all you have lost

and you will turn
toward it, let it bathe
your thirsty ears.

It could be an invisible
songbird, or a car rushing
by with the window down,

spilling out someone
else's soundtrack that one
split second you walk by.

You'll even stretch your
neck to find it, how
delicious this particular

mystery—some benevolent
party host leaving you
clues. How delicious

these five senses all—
each one a vine-covered
gate into the world outside

of thinking. Sometimes
it only takes a crack. You
wonder about the others—

why stop at only five?
What remains nameless has
led you to this very moment:

this song, these walking tears.
Your memory once a blade—
now a refuge, now a friend.

THE GHOST-ROAD

High praise for the art
of leaving—
it is so much harder
than it sounds.

A good Southerner can
stretch it out into a
bouquet of fragrant hours—
the lingering hugs, glasses
of sweet tea, *oh yes and
um-hmmm's, well I best
be on my way's* always
followed by someone
waving in the driveway
come back soon.

I prefer the warm comfort
of the sneak-out, the Irish
goodbye—slippers at my
door waiting, words on
nightstand pages so far
unread. I'll gladly take

the ghost-road without
the haunting—
and despite this riot
of loveliness,
disappear.

SWAN SONG CONTRAPUNTAL

My beloved skeleton   bent double
a toothless tiger   I am driving home
bathing in shadow   dust silent
ceremonially, nocturnally   seeking common language
There is a time limit   for what I feel
I have no savings account   for what I know
I offer one bright feather   for what we have lost
and dance away   never to return

HOME (ASH AND BONE)

When I die, burn
everything: words,
hair, body. Take me

to that valley, the
quiet one, and rest
there with your

face toward the sun
for just a moment.
Breathe in, hold it,

sigh. Find that spot
by the river—my
father will know, or

my young cousin—the
one where rippling water
bows along fence-line,

creates a shape we can
all agree is magnificent.
Pause there. Watch for

warblers in the brush,
bluebirds, on the banks:
dippers. Notice the wind.

See that spot where grand-
daddy trout lives tucked
deep into emerald green

below the curved bank—
sprinkle me there. Let
some ash fall in dancing

water, some on land.
(I smile thinking of
that bleached skeleton

I visit year after year,
ribcage collapsed into
gravity's soft geometry.)

Read some poems, of
course. Offer up a song
or two, give over a

melody to this sky right
here—this mountain,
then I will be home.

CIRCLE AT THE STILLPOINT

You unknow it for a while:
ladders appear and shout,
a confusion sets in deep like
a tattoo so that this great
forgetting becomes habitual,
ritual, inked in. And one day
sunlight beams in between
a curtain crack and directly on
to your grandmother's framed
face—even the dust seems
charged with possibility. Then
the next day you stumble upon
a deer in the most unlikely of
city backyard places, and she
looks up and out and through
you, and it is so profound you
wonder if you misunderstood.
A honeybee dances. A body
discards what it does not need.
Jasmine becomes a feast of
memory, fatherly woodsmoke
an invitation, invocation. Great
horned owl in silhouette joins
the conversation, then is gone.
An elder extends a hand caked
with dirt and grief and wisdom,
and suddenly it takes you back.
It was never not true. Suddenly
everything is holy all over again.

Author Bio

Beth Wood is an award-winning poet and singer-songwriter who has toured the country playing music and moving audiences for twenty-three years. Beth has released eleven solo albums, one duo project album, two books of poetry, and a collection of funny stories from the road. Beth's poetry book *Ladder To The Light* (Mezcalita Press) is the winner of the 2019 Oregon Book Awards People's Choice Award. Beth's work has expanded to include teaching and song coaching as well as leading workshops at festivals, songwriting retreats and beyond. Beth believes that engagement in the process of creation is as important as its outcome, and that there are no wrong notes.

MEZCALITA
PRESS

An independent publishing company
dedicated to bringing the printed poetry,
fiction, and non-fiction of musicians who
want to add to the power and reach
of their important voices.

CPSIA information can be obtained
at www.ICGtesting.com
Printed in the USA
BVHW031025270621
610586BV00008B/612

9 780999 478493